THIS BOOK
BELONGS TO

....

....

....

How to Use This Book

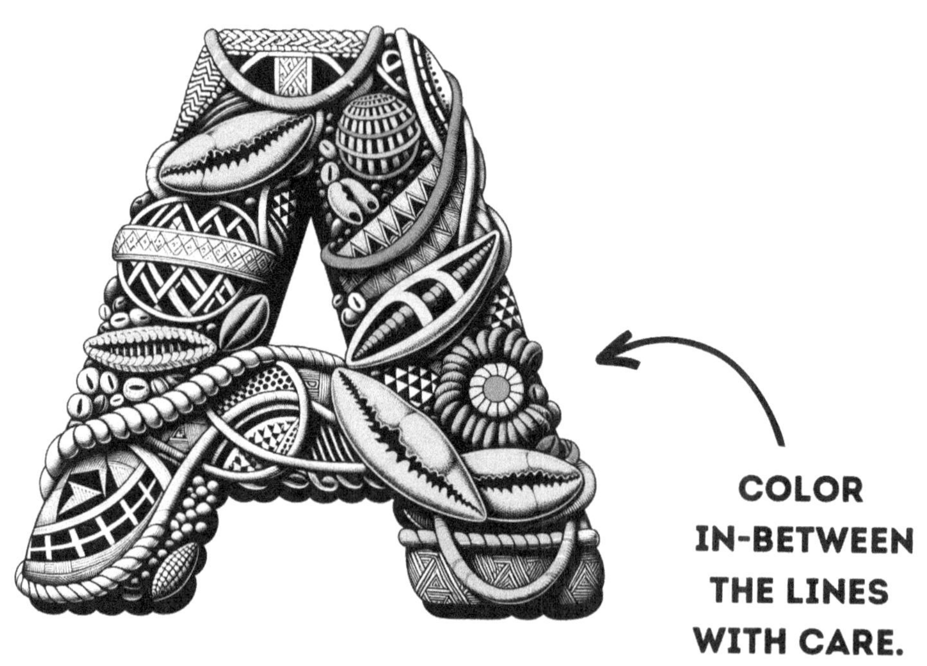

Get ready to be blown away by the stunning Cowry-themed Afrocentric TYPE FACE in this coloring book!.
Each letter of the alphabet has been transformed into a one-of-a-kind typeface design. With intricate details and patterns, this book is the perfect way to unleash your inner artist and dive into the world of coloring.
Let your imagination run wild as you experiment with different colors and shades, creating a masterpiece of your own.
Discover the magic of this breathtaking art form and let yourself be transported to a world of creativity and relaxation.

Test your Colour

intentionally left blank

ANCESTRY

Wrap your arms around the roots of Africa, where
shells once gleamed with significance, reminding us
that true riches go beyond mere money,
encompassing culture and heritage.

intentionally left blank

BOUNTY

Once upon a time, cowries reigned supreme as the ultimate cash kings. They flaunted wealth and prestige like nobody's business. But, let's pause for a second and let these tiny shells remind us that true treasures can be found in the most unassuming places.

intentionally left blank

COWRY

The cowry shell packs a punch: it whispers about power and prosperity that extend beyond plain old paper bills. Who knew that such a small and ancient artifact could still hold such sway today? It's a true gem of a find!

DURABILITY

"Let our wealth be as enduring as the cowry shell, empowering future generations to thrive!"

intentionally left blank

ESTEEM

Our culture is a goldmine of wealth, and it's crucial we treasure the customs that made us prosperous.

intentionally left blank

FLOURISH

Let's scatter the goodness like seashells across the shore, showering every community with blessings and lifting spirits high.

GRANDEUR

Our history is brimming with precious customs that pave the way for a future filled with riches. The traditions we carry are like shining stars, lighting the path to prosperity.

intentionally left blank

HERITAGE

Cowries - a nod to our heritage, where wealth was measured in wisdom and adventure.

INHERITANCE

Inheritance isn't just about the moolah and powerplay; it's an invaluable heirloom of traditions that withstands the test of time.

JOURNEY

Life's like a thrilling treasure hunt, every
stride gifting us with precious pearls of
tradition, strength, and prosperity.

KINSHIP

Kinship is the magical thread that weaves us together, fortifying our customs and honoring our roots. It's the cowries of connection that breathe life into our traditions.

intentionally left blank

LEGACY

"Let's leave our mark like the cowry shell, a
symbol of riches, influence, and heritage
that echoes for generations to come."

MAGNITUDE

"Our value isn't measured in small shells, but
in the might of our deeds and the depth of
our heritage."

NOBILITY

We embrace an illustrious way of life where
cowries embody the richness of character
and the might of heritage.

intentionally left blank

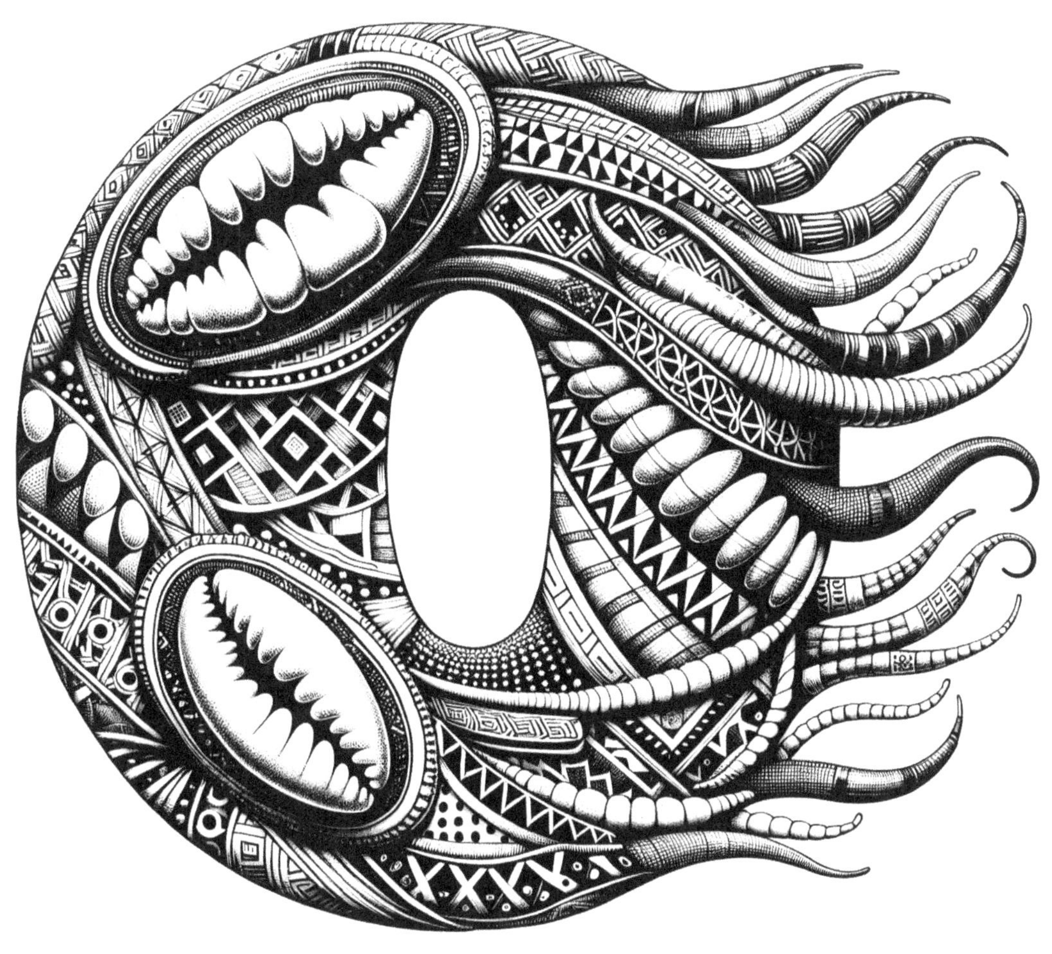

OPULENCE

Forget about piling up cowries, true wealth
is found in cherishing heritage and basking
in the glow of purposeful prosperity.

intentionally left blank

PROSPERITY

Let the humble cowries lead you to a world
of wealth, where tradition and modernity
blend in perfect harmony.

QUINTESSENCE

The cowry shell embodies the very essence
of olden riches, urging us to cherish our
roots with pride and might.

intentionally left blank

RESILIENCE

Let our riches stand the test of time, our might be fair and square, and our customs unshakable, like the mighty cowry shell.

SOVEREIGNTY

The cowry shell is a symbol of sovereignty, prosperity, and a way of life steeped in age-old traditions.

intentionally left blank

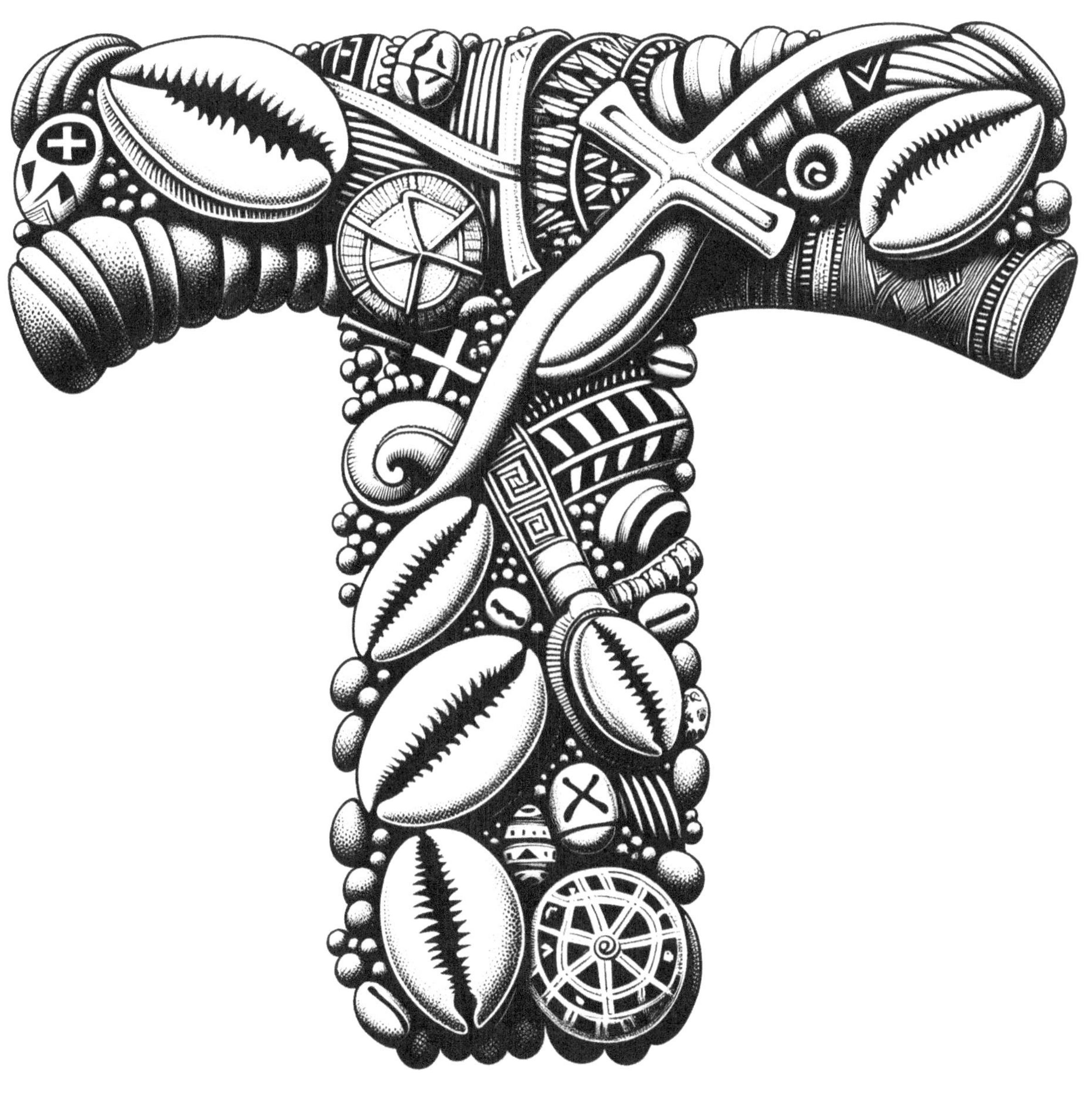

TIMELESSNESS

The humble cowry shell reminds us that
while riches and might may fade, customs
persevere, shaping who we are and how
we live.

UBIQUITY

The extensive utilization of cowries in ancient trade is a testament to humanity's unrelenting quest for wealth, power, and the upholding of long-standing traditions.

VIRTUE

"In the cowry, find virtue, and let it guide
your way of life, enriching your wealth,
empowering your spirit, and honoring
tradition."

WISDOM

Behold the mighty cowry! Despite its tiny size, it carries the weight of ancient wisdom, reminding us that true riches and might should coexist with the roots of our heritage.

intentionally left blank

EXPANSE

As the cowries spread across the oceans, they carry a message of abundance and generosity, reminding us that tradition and way of life thrive when wealth and power are shared.

YIELD

The cowrie yield shaped entire empires; how amazing would it be if our wealth and influence today were just as authentic, steeped in reverence for life and tradition.

ZEAL

Take a page from the cowry's book and
treasure the riches of simplicity, the
strength of tradition, and the wisdom of our
past.